EARLY ELEMENTARY

Sneezes, Snorts & Sniffles

7 PIANO PIECES WITH EXTRA-MUSICAL SOUNDS

BY WENDY STEVENS

ISBN 978-1-4803-9092-8

WILLIS MUSIC

EXCLUSIVELY DISTRIBUTED BY

HAL•LEONARD®
CORPORATION

7777 W. BLUEMOUND RD. P.O. BOX 13819 MILWAUKEE, WI 53213

Visit Hal Leonard Online at
www.halleonard.com

The Hiccup Song

Words and Music by
Wendy Stevens

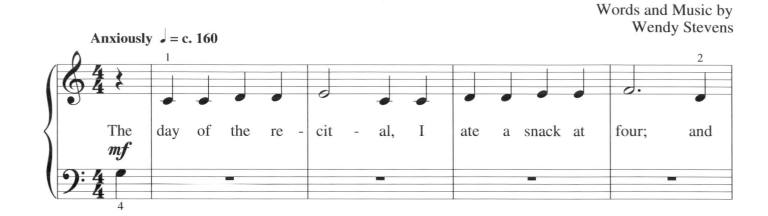

The day of the re - cit - al, I ate a snack at four; and

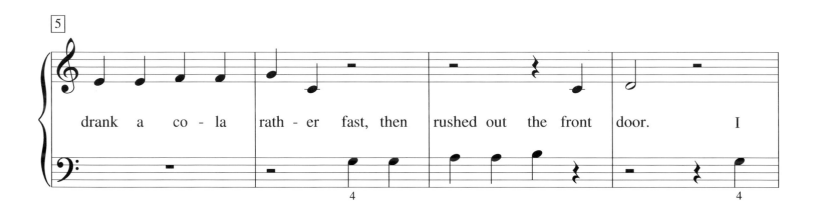

drank a co - la rath - er fast, then rushed out the front door. I

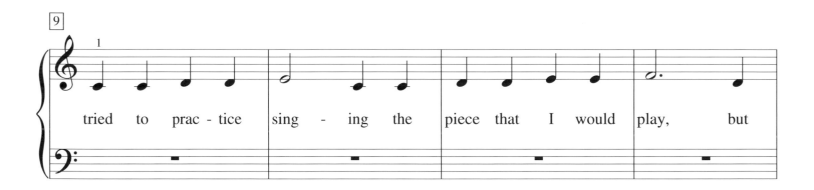

tried to prac - tice sing - ing the piece that I would play, but

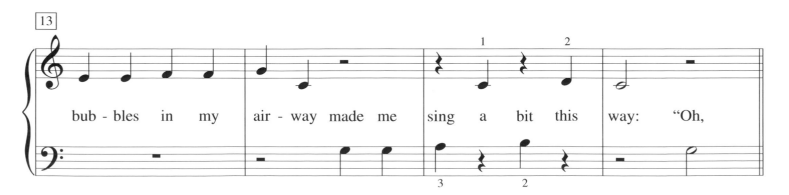

bub - bles in my air - way made me sing a bit this way: "Oh,

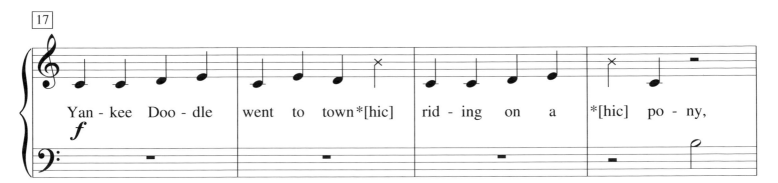

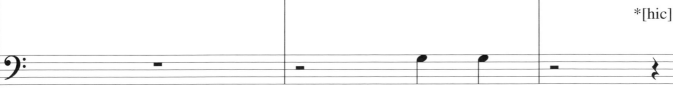

* Make a hiccup sound. If it is too difficult to sing the words and hiccup
  at the same time, just play the tune and hiccup where indicated.

4

Stinky Feet

Words and Music by
Wendy Stevens

Breathlessly ♩ = c. 168

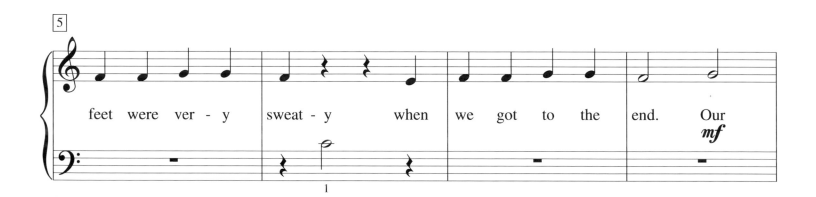

One day I was run - ning with all my dear - est friends. Our

feet were ver - y sweat - y when we got to the end. Our

run, it was a tough one, and we were ver - y sore but

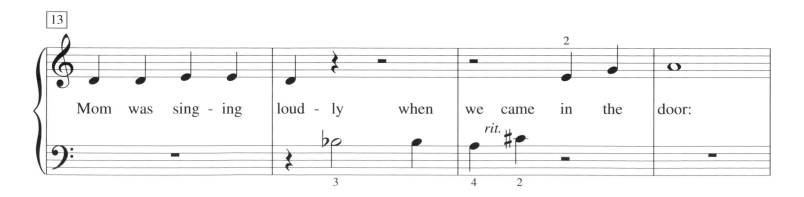

Mom was sing - ing loud - ly when we came in the door:

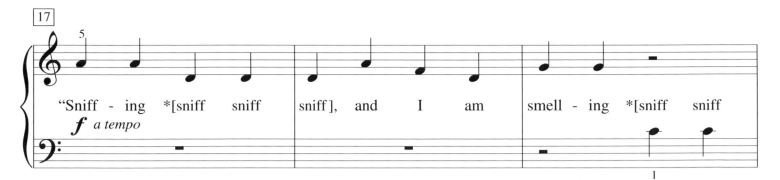

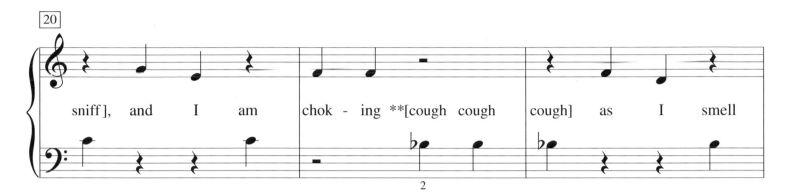

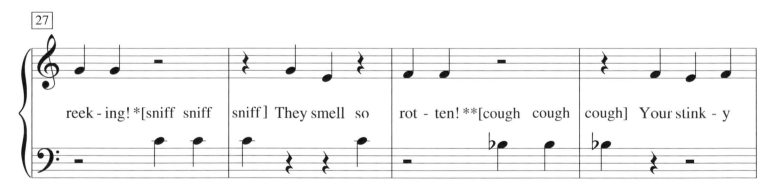

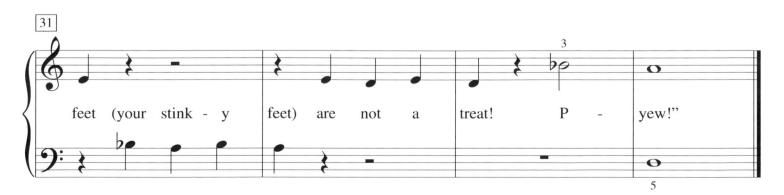

* *Make a sniffling sound with your nose.*
** *Cough out loud.*

A-choo!

Words and Music by
Wendy Stevens

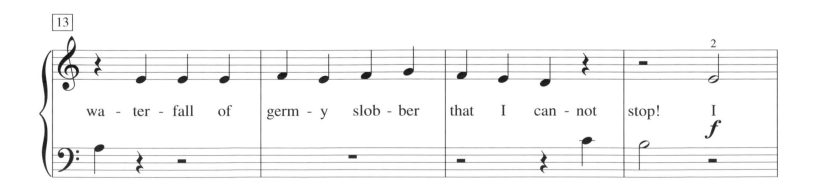

I felt good this morn - ing, and then with - out a warn - ing, my
nose be - came a tin - gly tun - nel for a piece of dirt. My
eyes are now a riv - er, I know I'll soon de - liv - er a
wa - ter - fall of germ - y slob - ber that I can - not stop! I

know I'll soon be   sneez - ing, there's no   way it will be   pleas - ing.   I

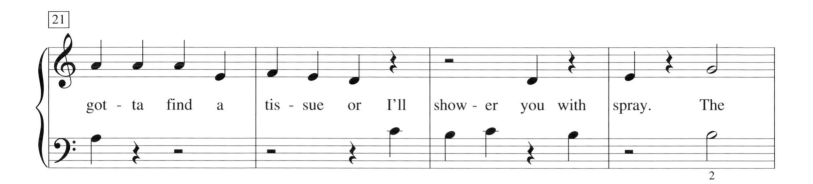

got - ta find a   tis - sue or I'll   show - er you with   spray.   The

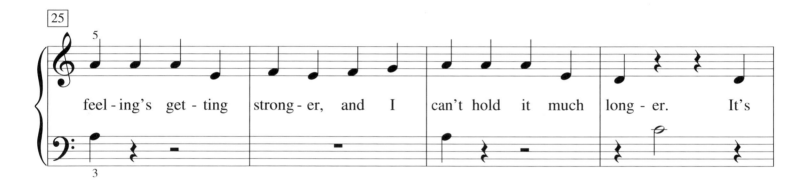

feel - ing's get - ting   strong - er, and I   can't hold it much   long - er.   It's

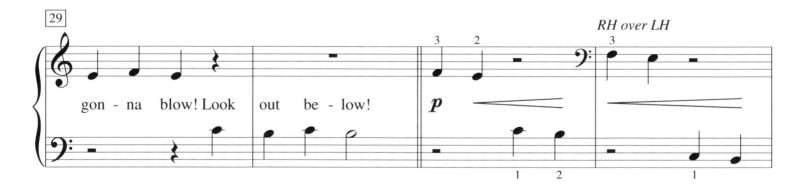

RH over LH

gon - na blow! Look   out be - low!   *p*

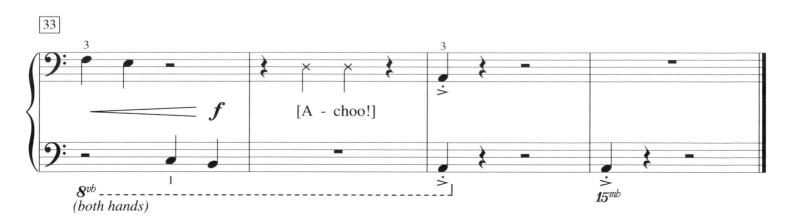

f   [A - choo!]

8vb -⌐
(both hands) 15^{mb}

I'll Give You a Snort

Words and Music by
Wendy Stevens

Happily ♩ = c. 168

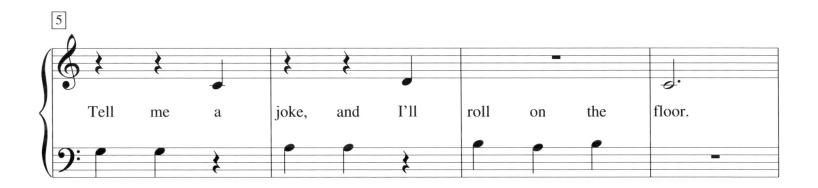

Tell me a joke, and I'll laugh till I'm cry - ing.

mp

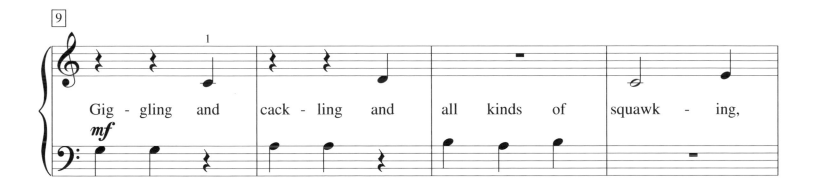

Tell me a joke, and I'll roll on the floor.

Gig - gling and cack - ling and all kinds of squawk - ing,

mf

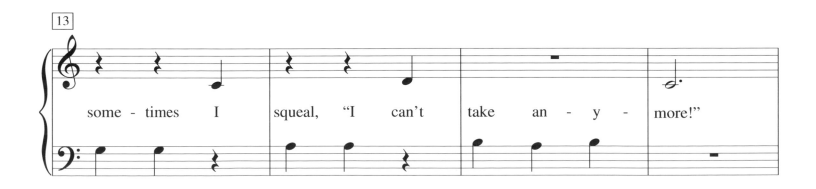

some - times I squeal, "I can't take an - y - more!"

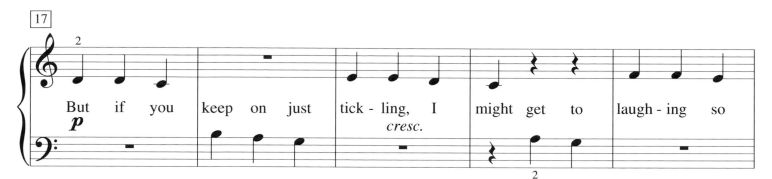

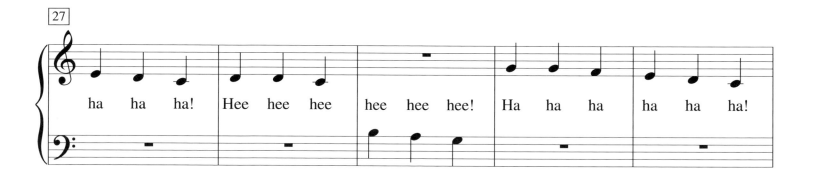

Make a snorting sound.

The Snoring Song

Words and Music by
Wendy Stevens

Steadily ♩ = c. 172

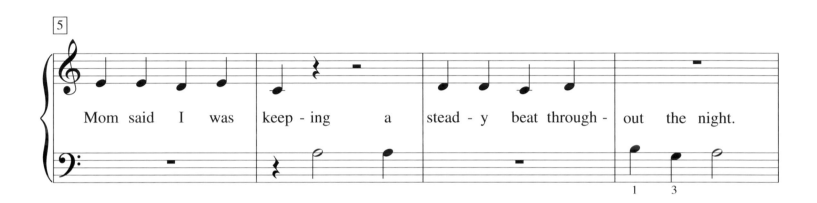

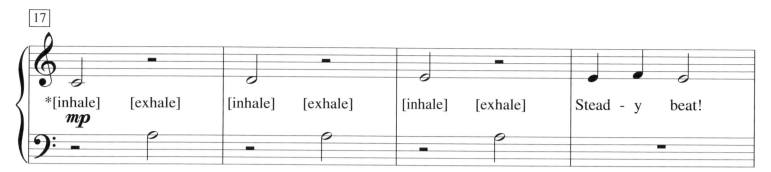

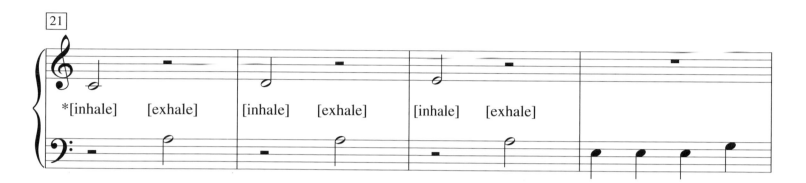

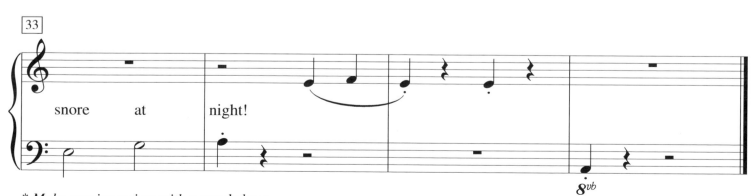

Make snoring noises with a steady beat.

The Gasping Song

Words and Music by
Wendy Stevens

Panicked! ♩ = c. 184

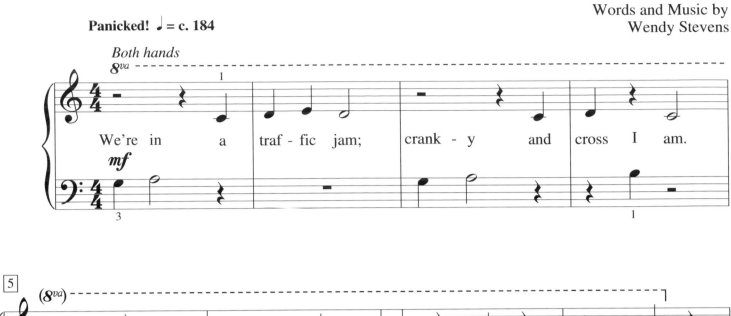

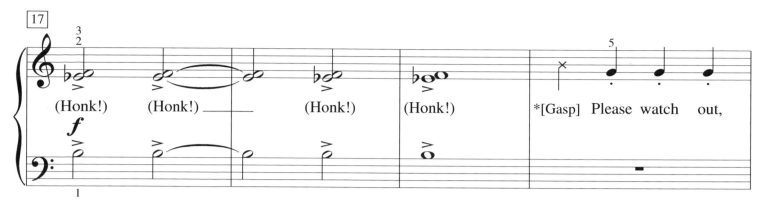

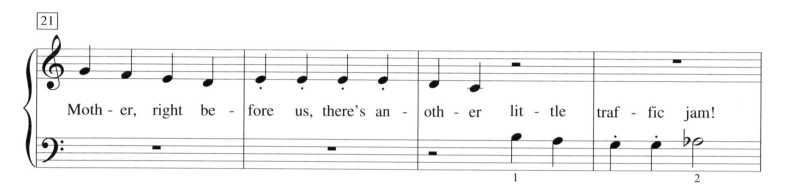

Play the top B and C on the piano

* Inhale suddenly as if you see something scary!

The Sniffles

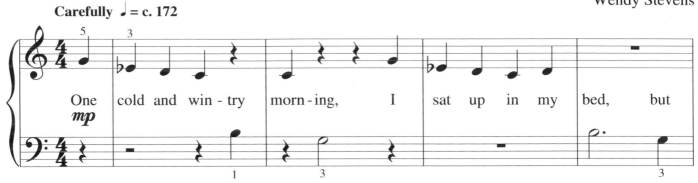

Words and Music by
Wendy Stevens

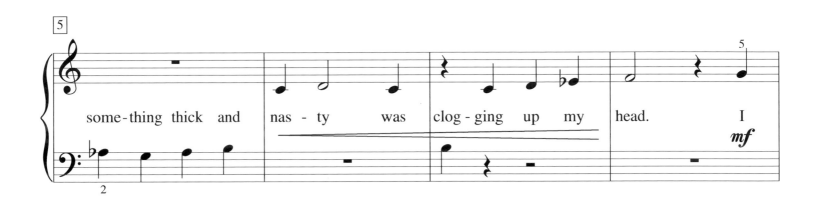

One cold and win-try morn-ing, I sat up in my bed, but

some-thing thick and nas-ty was clog-ging up my head. I

pulled my-self to-geth-er, I tried to get a grip but

when I was at break-fast, my nose be-gan to drip.

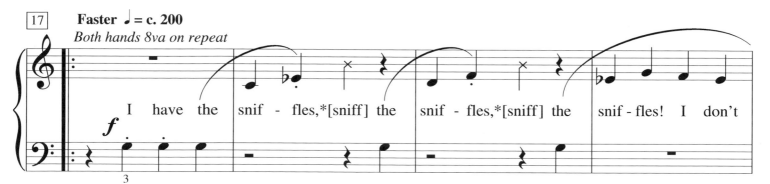

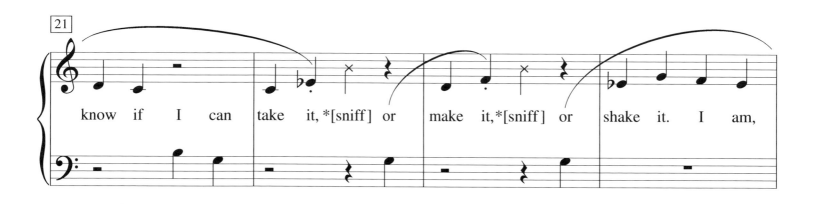

* Make a sniffling sound with your nose.

Wendy Stevens is a composer, pianist, teacher, and clinician. She received her Bachelor of Music in piano pedagogy and her Master of Music in theory and composition from Wichita State University. She has also taught theory at Wichita State and is a frequent adjudicator for music events in her area. In addition to her studio teaching, she has served as a church musician for over 20 years.

Wendy's piano workshops focus on creativity, composition, business practices, and technology. She maintains a popular blog for piano teachers at **www.ComposeCreate.com.**

MORE ELEMENTARY BOOKS BY WENDY STEVENS

Black Key Blast!
00123104

Presented especially for the youngest beginner, these easy, fun and motivating pieces using only the black keys will perk up any lesson, especially because students will be able to learn them almost immediately! With appealing titles such as "My Imaginary Friend," "I Am the Princess" and "Ninja Power," this collection (which comes with lyrics and accompaniments) should be a sure-fire hit in any studio.

Tasty Tunes
00121934

A delicious collection of food-inspired piano pieces for kids! Stevens' clever lyrics combined with her creative rhythmic nuances make this an engaging must-have for all teachers of early beginners. Titles include: I Love My Ranch • French Fries, Ice Cream • Macaroni Pizza • A Pickle Sandwich • Rock & Roll Rotini.